STEM JOBS IN
Movies

Carla Mooney

Educational Media

rourkeeducationalmedia.com

Scan for Related Titles
and Teacher Resources

Before Reading:

Building Academic Vocabulary and Background Knowledge

Before reading a book, it is important to tap into what your child or students already know about the topic. This will help them develop their vocabulary, increase their reading comprehension, and make connections across the curriculum.

1. *Look at the cover of the book. What will this book be about?*
2. *What do you already know about the topic?*
3. *Let's study the Table of Contents. What will you learn about in the book's chapters?*
4. *What would you like to learn about this topic? Do you think you might learn about it from this book? Why or why not?*
5. *Use a reading journal to write about your knowledge of this topic. Record what you already know about the topic and what you hope to learn about the topic.*
6. *Read the book.*
7. *In your reading journal, record what you learned about the topic and your response to the book.*
8. *After reading the book complete the activities below.*

Content Area Vocabulary
Read the list. What do these words mean?

animation
budget
coordinates
digital
hazardous
production
pyrotechnics
simulate
specialize
velocity
virtual

After Reading:

Comprehension and Extension Activity

After reading the book, work on the following questions with your child or students in order to check their level of reading comprehension and content mastery.

1. *Describe the role of STEM in the movie industry. (Summarize)*
2. *Why might a director use motion capture technology in a film? (Infer)*
3. *What special effects were used in a movie you've seen recently? (Text to self connection)*
4. *Describe how financial analysts use mathematics to make smart decisions about film production. (Summarize)*
5. *Describe how special effects have changed since movies that were made in the 1980s. (Visualize)*

Extension Activity

Create a six second video using the special effect of your choosing. Plan your materials, camera angles, and safety procedures necessary for your effect. Share your video with your friends or classmates.

Table of Contents

What Is Stem?

A computer animator creates a 3-D character for a feature film. A motion capture technician tracks an actor's movement via a computer program. A web developer creates an online portal where fans can watch movie trailers and learn the latest scoop about a movie studio's upcoming releases.

What do all these people have in common? It's not just movies! All their jobs require a STEM education. STEM is a shortcut for talking about science, technology, engineering, and mathematics.

PROD.NO.

SCENE	TAKE	SOUND

DIRECTOR

CAMERAMAN

DATE	EXT.	INT.

PRODUCED

Some of the most exciting careers are in STEM fields. A strong STEM education will allow you to research, test, and build new things. The problem-solving skills learned through STEM can take you to the next level in just about any career field. Find out more about the great STEM jobs that are waiting for you!

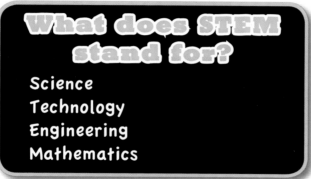

What does STEM stand for?

Science
Technology
Engineering
Mathematics

Computer Animation

Computer **animation** creates moving images and characters with the help of computers. Computer animation can be used to create a short commercial, a television show, a video game, or a full-length movie. Sometimes an entire film is animated. Other times, movies combine computer animation with real-life actors. Computer animators are needed to bring images to life on screen.

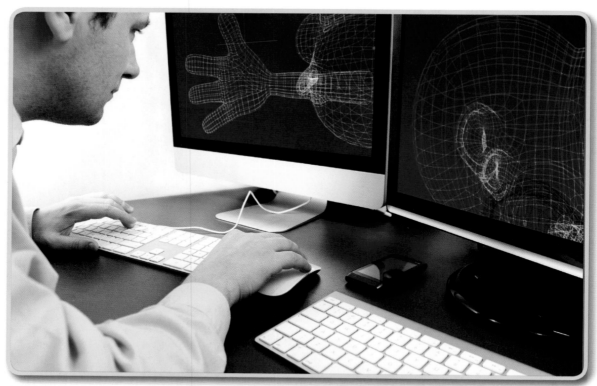

A computer animator uses special software to design a three-dimensional character.

To create a scene, computer animators begin with one picture called a frame. They change the next picture slightly. The following pictures are also changed slightly, one at a time. When flashed on a screen rapidly one after another, the frames create a moving image. An average computer-animated movie uses 25 frames per second.

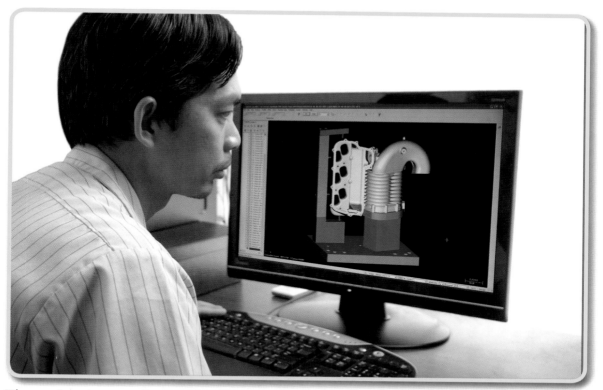

The animator studies and adjusts each frame in a project.

STEM in Action!

Geometry is a branch of math that studies shapes. Computer animators understand how shapes move when creating an animated scene. When a shape moves, it can be a turn, a flip, or a slide. Or in geometry terms, it can move as a rotation, a reflection, or a translation.

If a character needs to move a sword in a scene, how will it appear if the animator:

1. Rotates it?
2. Reflects it?
3. Translates it?

Often, a team of computer animators works on different parts of a movie. Some create a storyboard, a set of pictures that show what is going to happen in the movie. Others create characters. Some **specialize** in backgrounds and settings. When working on their part of the film, animators may spend hours perfecting the smallest details.

A storyboard shows what will happen in the movie. Animators follow a storyboard to create each scene in the movie or television show.

Most of today's computer animation is three-dimensional (3D). It has more depth and looks more realistic than 2D animation. To create 3D animation, a computer animator uses special modeling software. The animator creates a **virtual** model of a character. To make the character move, the animator moves the model. The animator figures out how to make the right movements and facial expressions by playing with the model.

Computer animators generate a three-dimensional car that will be inserted into a scene.

Real STEM Job: *Industrial Light and Magic Technical Animator*

Industrial Light and Magic is one of the world's leading effects companies. The company's animators have worked on hundreds of movies. Technical animators create the motion of computer-generated characters. From heroes to background creatures, vehicles, and props, technical animators do it all. They often work as part of a team.

These animators have advanced computer knowledge. Technical animators have studied computer science, computer visualization, or computer animation. They know how to use 3D computer animation software. They use this technology to create amazing things on screen.

When complete, the animated robot appears lifelike.

Motion Capture

Have you ever wondered how images made in a computer can look and act so lifelike? Motion capture technicians work with actors, **digital** cameras, and computers to create digital characters that look and act real.

Technicians attach reflective markers to an actor's legs. Each marker's position will be recorded as the actor moves.

Motion capture takes movements in real life and records them as a digital image. Movies use motion capture for computer-generated characters, creatures, and effects. For example, the movie *Avatar* used motion capture to create characters. Motion capture is also used to create movement in video games, such as *FIFA World Cup* and *Madden NFL*.

Characters from *Avatar* were generated using motion capture technology.

During a motion capture scene, an actor wears a special suit that is covered with small, reflective markers. Specialized cameras track the markers while the actor moves. The markers are recorded as 3D **coordinates**. Motion capture technicians use computer programs to collect the movement data and create motion for an animated image.

An actor wears a motion capture suit with reflective markers that will record his movements for technicians.

Real STEM Job: *DreamWorks Motion Capture Engineer*

DreamWorks has many motion capture technicians and engineers. They create the memorable characters seen in some of Hollywood's biggest movies. A DreamWorks engineer develops tools and procedures that turn a real-life scene into 3D animation. They set the stage for these shoots. During a shoot, they record data and set the actors in virtual sets.

This job requires knowledge of computer science or animation. Engineers have strong computer and artistic skills. They know about the human body, animation, and engineering. They are also skilled at computer programming and using special software. The engineers work closely with actors, technicians, artists, and other members on the film crew.

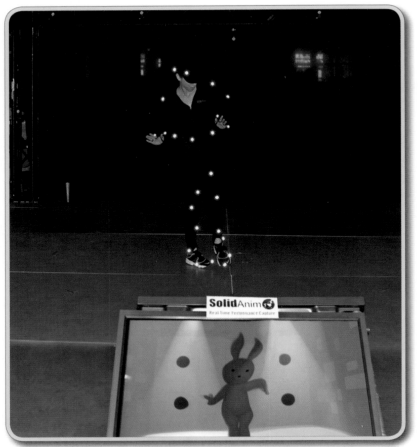

The more markers an actor wears, the more data points the motion capture technician has to create an animation.

Before filming, motion capture technicians work with the movie crew to decide what scenes need motion capture. Then they plan how and where they will record those pieces. On set, technicians fit actors with motion capture suits. They apply reflective markers to each subject. After filming, the technicians use computer programs to turn data they collected into an animated image. On the computer, they make the actor appear however they wish. They add skin, hair, tentacles, horns, limbs, clothing, and other effects. It takes many steps to create a living character using motion capture.

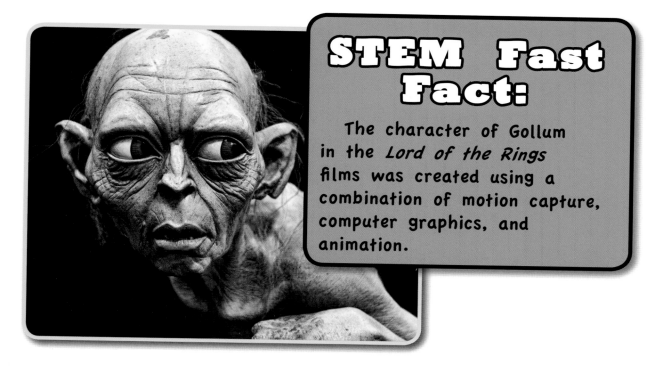

The character of Gollum in the *Lord of the Rings* films was created using a combination of motion capture, computer graphics, and animation.

STEM in Action!

Motion capture technicians use markers on reflective suits to record movement. The markers help them plot points on the actor's body in the computer.

Take a photo of a friend standing against a blank wall. Place the photo under graph paper and plot 10 points, such as feet, hands, knees, elbows, and head. Now have your friend strike a different pose. Plot those same points again.

How much did those points change? How might a computer use these points for motion capture technology?

Special Effects

On screen, a thrilling car chase ends when a car veers off the road, tumbles down a hillside, and explodes in an impressive fireball. To create this exciting chase, a film's special effects team works behind the scenes to make sure everything goes as planned and no one gets hurt.

Filmmakers work with special effects teams to create a car chase.

The special effects team makes sure no one gets hurt during the explosion.

Special effects are created on set during filming. Though the effects are done in a way that is safe for everyone on set, the explosions, crashes, and falls all really happened. Special effects occur when something is blown up, smashed, or destroyed on film. Special effects also create artificial rain, fog, smoke, and snow. **Pyrotechnics** and scale models are another part of special effects.

A controlled explosion occurs on a desert movie set.

The effects team plans and creates all the special effects in a film. The effects supervisor works with the film's **production** designer and art director to understand how they want the effects to look. The supervisor plans the necessary equipment, camera angles, and safety procedures.

On set, the special effects team works with many other members of the production team to design exciting and safe special effects.

Before filming, special effects technicians build and test the equipment that will create the effects. They use mechanical and electrical engineering concepts to create objects, buildings, and other structures. They handle explosives, high voltage, firearms, and other **hazardous** materials. On set, the special effects team makes sure the effects are done properly and safely.

Actors film a scene using effects built and tested by special effects engineers.

STEM in Action!

The special effects team uses physics to calculate how objects will move when planning special effects elements. When mapping out a car chase, the team needs to know how fast the stunt car will accelerate. Acceleration is the rate at which the **velocity** of an object changes. It is calculated as follows:

acceleration = change in velocity ÷ time

And to find the change in velocity, you would use the following equation:

change in velocity = final velocity - initial velocity

So, if a car goes from 0 to 60 miles per hour (mph) in 4 seconds, what is the acceleration?

First, use the equation to find the change in velocity:

60 - 0 = 60 mph

Now, find the acceleration:

60 ÷ 4 = 15 miles per second forward

The car moved forward at 15 miles per second!

STEM Spotlight

For one scene in the movie *National Treasure 2*, the production team needed to design waterfalls. To create this special effect, they turned to special effects engineers. The special effects engineers designed and built three large rectangular steel ducts to **simulate** waterfalls at Universal Studios Falls Lake. The engineers also designed and built a wooden support structure to hold the water ducts in place. The support structure had to be made specially so that it could withstand the forces from the flowing water.

Financial Analysis

Movie studios spend millions of dollars to create blockbuster films. How do they know if they have made any money on the film? Financial analysts and accountants track how much a film costs and how much it earns.

Before a film begins, financial analysts work with the production team to create a **budget**. They predict what a film's costs are going to be. Using a computer, they also build financial models. The team uses the models to compare different ways they can make the movie. To keep costs low, they may choose to use less expensive equipment. Or they may schedule more scenes to be shot in one day. The models help them decide the best way to move forward.

Financial analysts create a film's budget and use it to make buying decisions.

Real STEM Job: *Production Financial Analyst at Walt Disney Studios*

Production financial analysts at Walt Disney Studios work as part of the production team. They help the studio understand how money is being spent. They look at how much work is done on the film to understand if money is being well spent. Every week, the analyst reviews a project's progress and compares it to the schedule. The analyst also prepares reports for the studio's senior leaders.

This job requires strong math and analytical skills. Analysts have studied finance and accounting. They use computer programs, such as Excel, PowerPoint, and other accounting software. They also have sharp attention to detail.

During a project, financial analysts compare actual results to the projected budget. They explain any differences. Was shooting delayed because of bad weather? Did a special effect cost more than expected? They decide if the project is making good progress based on its budget. Financial analysts will update the models and schedules as the project progresses.

A financial analyst reviews production costs and compares it to projections.

STEM in Action!

A film's budget estimates $100,000 for set construction. The actual bills are as follows:

Materials: $75,000
Labor: $30,000
Insurance: $10,000

Did the film run over or under budget for set construction? By how much?

Total spent: $75,000 + $30,000 + $10,000 = $115,000

Variance: Actual - Budget: $115,000 - $100,000 = $15,000

The film went over budget by $15,000. To make up for this spending, the financial analyst will look through the budget to find other areas where they could spend less money.

Financial analysts also prepare reports to share with senior management. Using PowerPoint and other computer programs, they create presentations to highlight important information. Executives need this information to make smart decisions.

Visual Effects

Visual effects are an important part of today's movie making. Almost every film you watch will have some type of visual effects. Unlike special effects, which are filmed on set, visual effects are added later using computers. Explosions, floods, 3D models, scenery, and backgrounds are often added digitally. Visual effects are used to add things that would be too difficult or expensive to create in live action.

When planning a film, the visual effects team designs rough sketches, paintings, animations, or models. They work with the film's director and producer to decide what effects to use in the movie. They plan when blue or green screens and other equipment will be used in filming.

Filmmakers often use green screens because they are the color that is furthest way from natural skin tones. This makes it easy to remove the green in a computer without affecting the way the actor looks.

STEM Fast Fact:

Sometimes actors are filmed in front of a blue or green screen. Later, the visual effects team adds a completely different background to the scene.

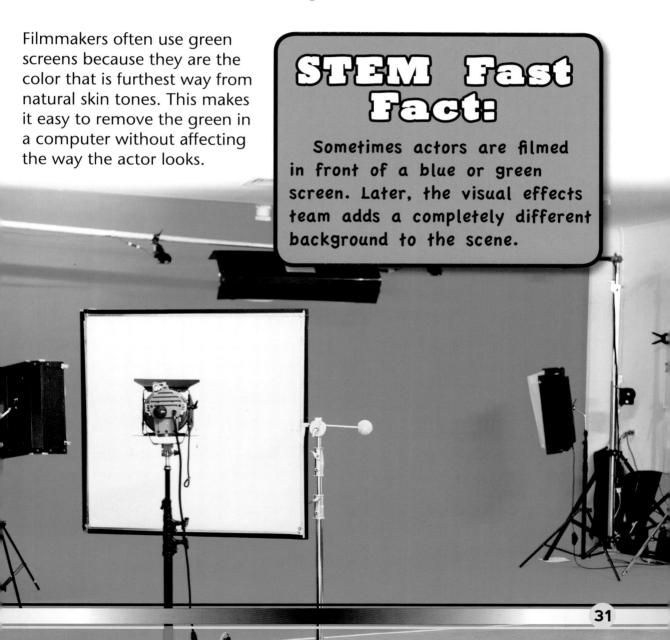

On set, the visual effects team (VFX) makes sure the proper sight lines, lighting, and framing are used during filming. Scenes must be filmed properly for them to add the visual effects later. The visual effects team uses computers to add digital elements to the scenes. They create a snowy landscape for a holiday movie. They add a thousand warriors to a battle scene. They create fire-breathing dragons that soar through the air, setting villages on fire. Other times, the VFX team will remove elements from a scene, such as erasing a building from the background of a scene.

Visual effects make this actress appear as if she is floating in space.

STEM in Action!

The visual effects team uses the relationship between light and distance to create accurate lighting on a shot of a CGI character. The team uses the following table:

Distance	Light Intensity
30 inches	1 lumen
60 inches	0.241 lumens
90 inches	0.117 lumens
120 inches	0.060 lumens

If an object is moved from a distance of 30 inches to a distance of 90 inches, how should the team adjust the digital lighting to make the scene as realistic as possible?

They should adjust the light intensity to 0.117 lumens.

Proper lighting helps make a CGI character appear realistic.

Real STEM Job:
FX Technical Director

FX technical directors create particle, body, fluid, cloth, fur, and hair simulations. They also make realistic digital effects like smoke, fire, clouds, water, steam, and explosions. Computer software products including Houdini, Maya, and in-house tools help bring their effects to life on screen.

This job requires strong math, science, engineering, and computer skills. FX technical directors combine technical skills with creativity. They have an eye for detail, but also understand how to use technology to make their visions a reality.

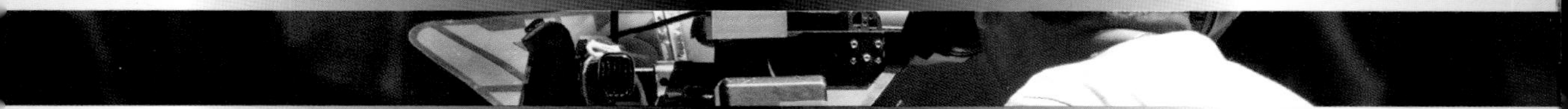

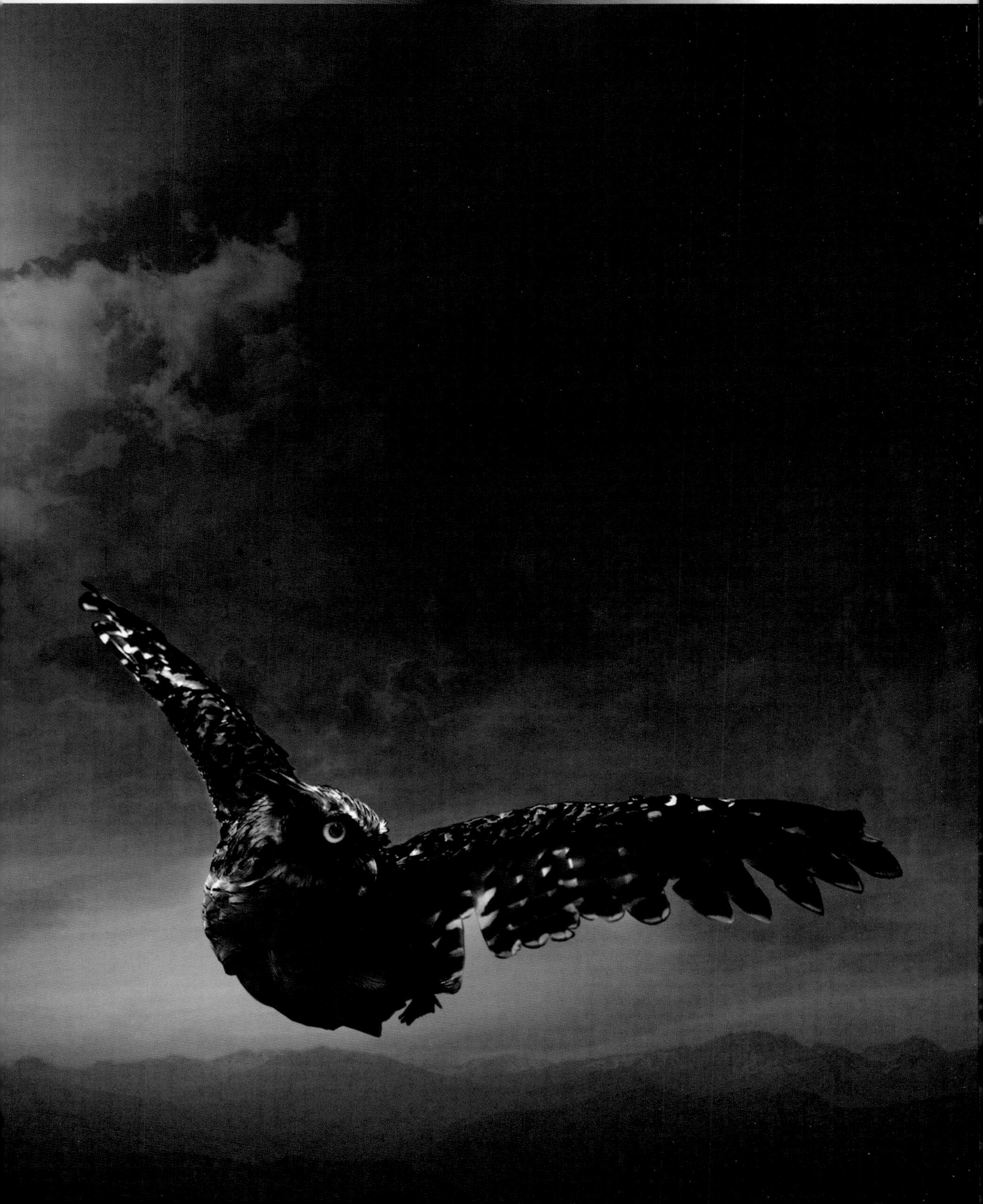

Web Development

Almost everyone in the entertainment industry today has a website. Studios promote actors, films, videos, and television shows. Fans visit a studio's website to learn more about current films and upcoming projects. Designing a website that is creative and attractive to fans is the job for web developers.

Web developers create specialized, eye-catching websites for the film industry. Web developers use color, images, layouts, photos, and fonts to create sites that showcase different films.

Because every film is different, web developers work to create a site that reflects the film's needs. Some movies want to show trailers and clips of their movies. Others want to share reviews. Some websites do not want to spoil the plot of the movie. Instead, they create games that will get viewers excited about the film.

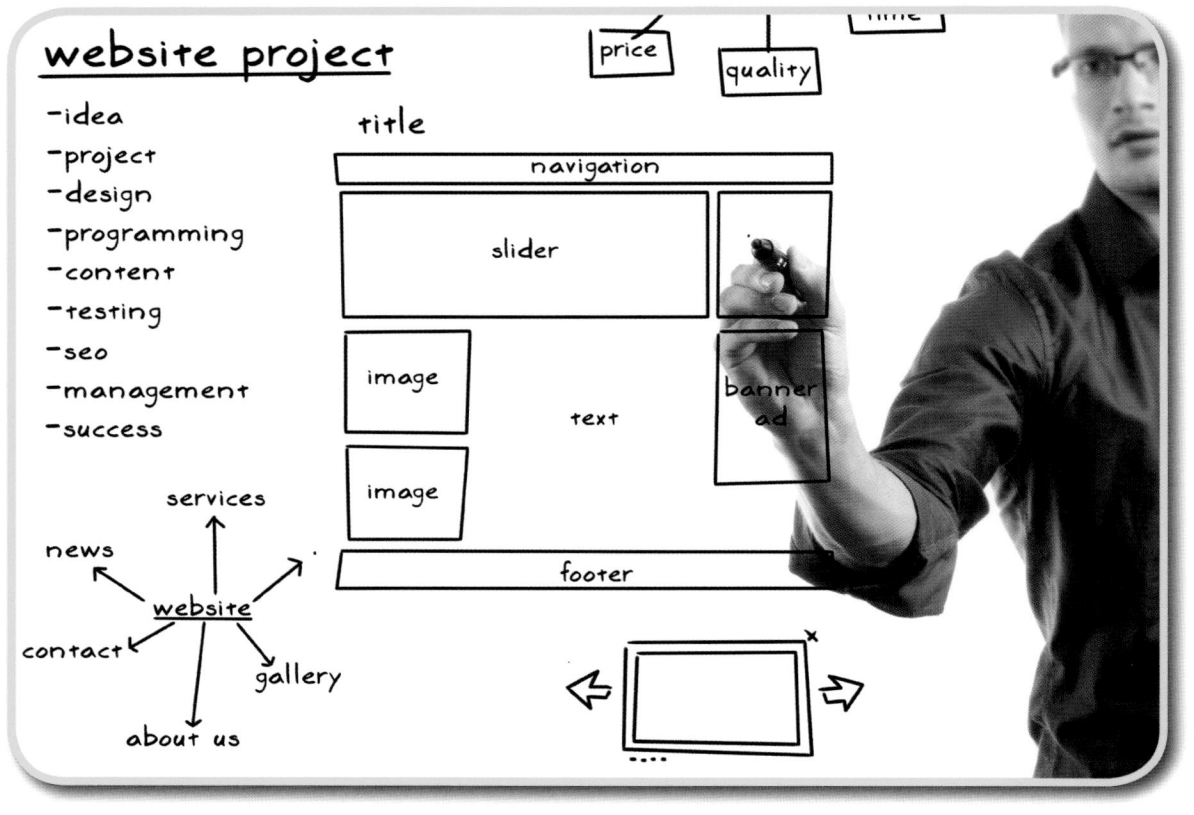

Before building a website, a developer designs the elements on each web page.

```html
<!DOCTYPE HTML>
<html>
<head>
<meta http-equiv="Content-Type" content=
<title>SITE - Home</title>
<style type="text/css">
<!--
body {
font:  100%/1.4  Verdana, Geneva, Arial,
background: #1C3664;
margin: 0;
padding: 0;
color: #666;
font-size:13px;


}
h2 {font-size:13px}
/* ~~ Element/tag selectors ~~ */
ul, ol, dl { /* Due to variations between br
padding: 0;
margin: 0;

                h3, h4, h5, h6, p {
  h2, h3, h4,        /* removing the top margi
margin-top                    ding the paddin
            ight: 15px;
```

STEM in Action!

Web developers know how to use HTML coding to build websites. HTML stands for HyperText Markup Language. It is the language used to create web pages that can be displayed in a web browser. HTML uses tags to mark blocks of text on a page. One of the most common HTML tags used is the <strong> or bold tag. It is used to mark text that should be bolded. For example, <STRONG>THIS IS BOLD TEXT</STRONG>.

How would a developer code the following sentence to make the words "Avengers" bold?

New Avengers movie to be released in August.

It would be coded as follows:
NEW <STRONG>AVENGERS</STRONG> MOVIE TO BE RELEASED IN AUGUST.

The code would appear on the website as:
New **Avengers** movie to be released in August.

Real STEM Job: *FilmTrack Web Developer*

FilmTrack is a leading provider of websites for entertainment companies. Its web developers design, create, and implement websites. Working with other team members, they design company websites from the idea stage to a working site. They use computer skills to build, maintain, and troubleshoot the sites.

This job requires strong computer skills and experience in web design. Developers are skilled at web programming using HTML and CSS. They know how to use computer programs such as Adobe Photoshop, Flash FTP, and Microsoft Project. For someone who enjoys both computers and movies, this job may be the perfect combination!

Web developers decide which photos to use on a website for an upcoming movie release.

STEM Careers

Some of the most exciting careers in movies are in STEM fields. Jobs in computer animation, special effects, motion capture, visual effects, and web development are just some examples of movie careers that use STEM skills every day. The skills you learn from STEM subjects can be a great foundation for almost any career you choose!

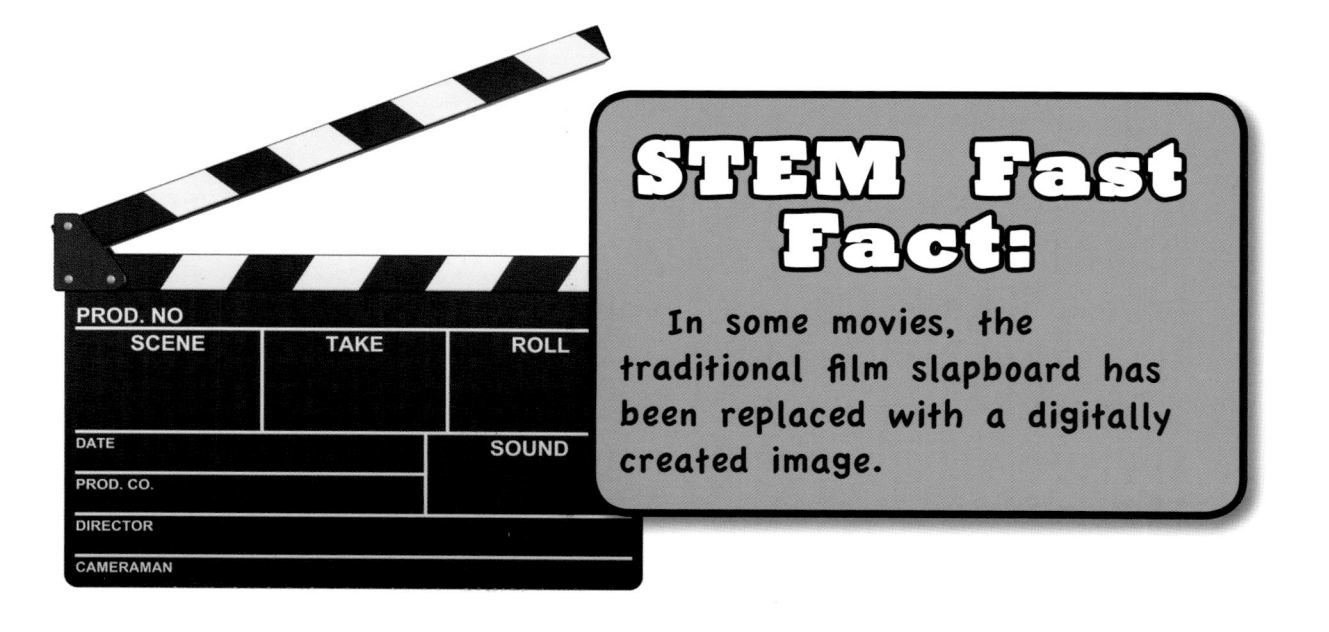

Without contributions from STEM jobs, today's movies would not be complete!

PROD.
| ROLL | SCENE | TAKE |
| 8 | 9F | 3 | -3 |
DIRECTOR
CAMERA
DATE / /   NIGHT INT   MOS
S.D.   FILTER

PROD. NO		
SCENE	TAKE	ROLL
DATE		SOUND
PROD. CO.		
DIRECTOR		
CAMERAMAN		

STEM Fast Fact:

In some movies, the traditional film slapboard has been replaced with a digitally created image.

STEM Job Fact Sheets

Computer Animator

Important Skills: Advanced Computer Skills, Mathematics, Animation

Important Knowledge: Computer Programming, Understanding of Light, Color, Texture, Creativity

College Major: Computer Science, Computer Animation

Median Salary: $61,370

Motion Capture Technician

Important Skills: Advanced Computer Skills, Artistic, Interpersonal Skills

Important Knowledge: Biomechanical, Engineering, Animation, Motion Capture, Animation Software

College Major: Computer Animation, Media Arts and Animation, Graphic Design

Median Salary: $61,370

Special Effects Supervisor

Important Skills: Electrical Engineering, Mechanical Engineering, Film Production, Hazardous Materials

Important Knowledge: Advanced Mathematics, Physics, Chemistry, Local Regulations of Firearms and Hazardous Materials

College Major: Engineering, Film and Television Production

Median Salary: $62,000

Film Financial Analyst

Important Skills: Accounting, Mathematics, Analytical Skills, Writing Skills

Important Knowledge: Mathematics, Entertainment Industry, Computer Software Packages

College Major: Accounting, Finance, Mathematics

Median Salary: $76,950

FX Technical Director

Important Skills: Advanced Computer Skills, Advanced Mathematical Skills, Strong Communication, Problem-Solving Skills

Important Knowledge: Software Design, Programming, Animation Software Tools, Advanced Mathematics, Science, Engineering

College Major: Computer Science, Computer Animation

Median Salary: $106,080

Web Developer

Important Skills: Computers, Web Skills, Design, Creativity

Important Knowledge: HTML, JavaScript, Adobe Photoshop, Flash, CSS

College Major: Computer Science

Median Salary: $62,500

Glossary

animation (an-uh-MAY-shuhn): a film made by projecting a series of drawings very quickly so that the objects in the drawings appear to move

budget (BUHJ-it): a plan for how money will be earned and spent

coordinates (koh-OR-duh-nitz): a set of numbers used to show the position of a point on a line, graph, or map

digital (DIJ-uh-tuhl): a form that can be used by a computer

hazardous (HAZ-ur-duhss): dangerous or risky

production (pruh-DUHK-shuhn): a form of entertainment that is presented to others, such as a play or movie

pyrotechnics (pahy-ruh-TEK-niks): the art of making fireworks

simulate (sim-yuh-leyt): to pretend to be or create a model of something

specialize (SPESH-uh-lize): to focus on one specific area of expertise; made for a specific purpose

velocity (VUH-los-i-tee): the rate of speed

virtual (VUR-choo-uhl): something that is simulated on a computer

Index

Show What You Know

1. What does STEM stand for?
2. What STEM skills are used in movie making?
3. How is science used in special effects?
4. What type of computer science jobs can be found at a movie studio?
5. What characteristics does a successful web developer need to have?

Websites to Visit

www.bls.gov

www.getinmedia.com

stemcareer.com

About the Author

Carla Mooney has written many books for children and young adults. She lives in Pennsylvania with her husband and three children. She enjoys learning about how science can be used in a variety of areas and careers.

Meet The Author!
www.meetREMauthors.com

www.rourkeeducationalmedia.com

PHOTO CREDITS: Cover © adventtr, small_frog, powerofforever, Tatiana Morozocval/Shutterstock; Title Page © dabldy; page 4 © Africa Studio; page 5 © Goodluz; page 6 © small_frog; page 7 © Chuck Rausin; page 8 © Vector Shots; page 9 © KUCO; page 10 © Scott Betts; page 11 © higyou; page 12 © D.Gordon E. Robertson; page 13 © Twin Design; page 14 © garymilner; page 15 © CountryStyle Photography; page 16 © Dalbéra J.P.; page 17 © Alan Crosthwaite; page 18 © robocoquyt, splain2me; page 19 © CREATISTA; page 20 © FlashStudio; page 21 © Eniko Balogh; page 23 © San-Spek; page 24 © Robert Kneschke, koya979; page 25, 26 © Dragon Images; page 27 © Nonwarit; page 29 © Zsolt Nyulaszi; page 30 © vicnt; page © Steve Lovegrove; page 32 © Andre Nosov; page 33 © Janaka Dharmasena; page 34 © Krisosheev Vitaly; page 36 © Andrey_Popov; page 37 © ronstik; page 38 © SoulArt; page 41 © Yuri Arcurs; page 42 © V. Kreinacke; page 43 © bjones27, angelhell

Edited by: Jill Sherman

Cover design by: Tara Raymo
Interior design by: Renee Brady

Library of Congress PCN Data

STEM Jobs in Movies / Carla Mooney
(STEM Jobs You'll Love)
ISBN 978-1-62717-701-6 (hard cover)
ISBN 978-1-62717-823-5 (soft cover)
ISBN 978-1-62717-937-9 (e-Book)
Library of Congress Control Number: 2014935494

Printed in the United States of America, North Mankato, Minnesota

Also Available as: